Tap the
Puck

PHASE 2

/ck/
/e/u/

Level 1 – Pink

BookLife

9112000538365

Helpful Hints for Reading at Home

The graphemes (written letters) and phonemes (units of sound) used throughout this series are aligned with Letters and Sounds. This offers a consistent approach to learning whether reading at home or in the classroom.

HERE IS A LIST OF NEW PHONEMES FOR THIS PHASE OF LEARNING. AN EXAMPLE OF THE PRONUNCIATION CAN BE FOUND IN BRACKETS.

Phase 2			
s (sat)	a (cat)	t (tap)	p (tap)
i (pin)	n (net)	m (man)	d (dog)
g (go)	o (sock)	c (cat)	k (kin)
ck (sack)	e (elf)	u (up)	r (rabbit)
h (hut)	b (ball)	f (fish)	ff (off)
l (lip)	ll (ball)	ss (hiss)	

HERE ARE SOME WORDS WHICH YOUR CHILD MAY FIND TRICKY.

Phase 2 Tricky Words			
the	to	I	no
go	into		

TOP TIPS FOR HELPING YOUR CHILD TO READ:

• Allow children time to break down unfamiliar words into units of sound and then encourage children to string these sounds together to create the word.

• Encourage your child to point out any focus phonics when they are used.

• Read through the book more than once to grow confidence.

• Ask simple questions about the text to assess understanding.

• Encourage children to use illustrations as prompts.

PHASE 2
/ck/
/e/ /u/

This book focuses on the phonemes /ck/, /e/ and /u/ and is a pink level 1 book band.

Can you say this sound and draw it with your finger?

It is a puck.

It is a net.

Tap the puck.

Tap it to the net.

Tap tap tap!

Go go go!

Tap the puck.

It is in the net!

©2021 **BookLife Publishing Ltd.**
King's Lynn, Norfolk PE30 4LS

ISBN 978-1-83927-895-2

Tap the Puck
Written by William Anthony
Designed by Jasmine Pointer

An Introduction to BookLife Readers...

Our Readers have been specifically created in line with the London Institute of Education's approach to book banding and are phonetically decodable and ordered to support each phase of the Letters and Sounds document.

Each book has been created to provide the best possible reading and learning experience. Our aim is to share our love of books with children, providing both emerging readers and prolific page-turners with beautiful books that are guaranteed to provoke interest and learning, regardless of ability.

BOOK BAND GRADED using the Institute of Education's approach to levelling.

PHONETICALLY DECODABLE supporting each phase of Letters and Sounds.

EXERCISES AND QUESTIONS to offer reinforcement and to ascertain comprehension.

CLEAR DESIGN to inspire and provoke engagement, providing the reader with clear visual representations of each non-fiction topic.

AUTHOR INSIGHT:
WILLIAM ANTHONY

Despite his young age, William Anthony's involvement with children's education is quite extensive. He has written over 60 titles with BookLife Publishing so far, across a wide range of subjects. William graduated from Cardiff University with a 1st Class BA (Hons) in Journalism, Media and Culture, creating an app and a TV series, among other things, during his time there.

William Anthony has also produced work for the Prince's Trust, a charity created by HRH The Prince of Wales, that helps young people with their professional future. He has created animated videos for a children's education company that works closely with the charity.

PHASE 2

/ck/
/e/u/

This book focuses on the phonemes /ck/, /e/ and /u/ and is a pink level 1 book band.

Image Credits Images are courtesy of Shutterstock.com. With thanks to Getty Images, Thinkstock Photo and iStockphoto. Cover – Lucky Businessw, Tatiana Popova, Iasha. 4 – Vaclav Volrab. 5 – Shooter Bob Square Lenses. 6 – Ronnie Chua. 7 – Domenic Gareri. 8 – Ronnie Chua. 9 – dotshock. 10 – Iurii Osadchi. 11 – Shooter Bob Square Lenses.

BookLife Non-Fiction Readers

9781839278938

9781839278921

9781839278945

9781839278952

9781839278976

9781839278969

9781839278990

9781839278983

9781839279010

9781839279003

9781839279027

9781839279034

9781839279058

9781839279041

EXPLORE A WORLD OF NON-FICTION WITH OUR DECODABLE READER RANGE

MORE COMING SOON

BookLife PUBLISHING

BookLife Readers

The BookLife Readers begin with the very basics of **phonetically decodable reading**. Starting with the earliest step of **CVC** words – words comprising a consonant, a vowel and a consonant – and building on this combination slowly, the reader follows a prescribed format taken directly from the recognised **Letters and Sounds** educational document.

By aligning our books with Letters and Sounds, we offer our readers a consistent approach to learning, whether at home or in the classroom. Books levelled as 'a' are an introduction to the band. Readers can advance to 'b' where graphemes are consolidated and further graphemes are introduced. The illustrations guide the reader, helping to deliver reading progression through the scheme in a **colourful** and **exciting** way. As a reader moves through the book band levels, the page numbers, level of repetition and sentence structure complexity all advance at a rate which **encourages development** without halting enjoyment.

To find out more about this exciting new reading scheme, visit www.booklife.co.uk

BookLife Readers

Our BookLife Readers include activities, quizzes and learning resources perfect for the home or classroom environment.

Can you draw the focus sound with your finger?

Hairy Fairy Ears

1. Where do the fairies live?

2. How did Azure's hairy e

3. What did the witch w
   (a) Cut them off
   (b) Pull out the
   (c) Tickle then

What did Tessa

How would y
change your

Can you make it through the maze to collect the letter z? How many objects beginning with z can you collect along the way?

Can you draw the focus sound with your finger?

Can you draw the focus sound with your finger?

BookLife
PUBLISHING